OTHER
/
WISE

BY THE SAME AUTHOR

POETRY

Fistful of Lotus (Elizabeth Forrest, 2000)
Home Test (Adastra Press, 2009)

PROSE

Quiet Accomplishment: Remembering Cid Corman
(Ekstasis Editions, 2014)

Contents

I

Ferris Wheel	13
Seed Trees	14
Earl's Sauna	16
At Twenty	17
Talking to Water	20
Dream Song	22
Watching the Dancers Carrying Their Shoes Home	23
In Reply to the English Professor Who Warned His His Teaching Assistants Never to Date a Student	25
Small Beer	26
Vocation	27
Leaving a Forest	29

II

Ikebana	33
Omi-Ai	34
Along the Kamo	36
In Praise of the Hot Japanese Summer	37
No Hands	39
Girl on Fence	40
Learning Better	42
Hanami	45
Visiting	46
'Frosted pickle barrels'	48
Treasure	49
Hirosato	52
Elegy for Autumn Gordon, 14 Years	54

III

Throwing My Life Away	57
What Is Great	58
Kae's Vision	59
Walking Home	60
The Dance	62
Finders Keepers	63
Like a Poem	64
Points of Departure	66
Skylight	69
Drifting	70
Home Test	72
First Day	73
Notes	77

In Noh drama the actor indicates a journey, even a lengthy journey, by standing in one spot and turning himself in a full circle. Thus we see in this simplest of gestures, that points of departure and of arrival are one and the same.

from *The Gates of Night, Six Songs from the* NOH
— David Jenkins *&* Yasuhiko Moriguchi

Poetry becomes
that conversation we
could not otherwise have.

– Cid Corman

for Cid & Shizumi
& David Jenkins
in memory

I

well which way
go
with the wind blowing

– Santōka

Ferris Wheel

> *the journey itself is home*
> — Bashō

Belinda, we were just kids
saying goodbye,
trying to imagine what it'd be like
never to see each other again.
And we felt that
and sought a way
to say goodbye – so went
to the carnival, enjoyed the rides
and later walked into a prairie
where we could exhaust every last word
and fall into each other's arms,
for what we were learning was all
that could be said finally, kisses,
and more kisses, then rolling
over the ground until
the carnival was nothing but a few
lights flickering on and off
like the last embers of a fire
we might have called childhood,
for when we stood and walked away
from that field, that night,
our lives were opening out
past the lights flooding
broken over puddles, past
the beginning of rain,
into the dark and glistening
streets leading us home.

Seed Trees

– for William Stafford, in memory

His wife spoke of his readiness
to drop anything
at a moment's notice – his readiness
to run and help a neighbor
who might have given him a call.

His response was always the same:
Be right there! Imagine
the presence of mind –
so prepared as that –
to say whatever I am doing now

can wait until I see about you first.
Maybe he *was* a genius
as Jonathan Holden said,
a man who made his poems
with pleasure and ease,

but her quavering voice tells me,
he was also someone who understood
how many a poem remains –
because it was left
along the way – unwritten

to do its work in time
the way a logger might
plant the finest trees
by leaving one behind –
the tallest strongest one –

to seed the forest back again alive.

Mt. Hood National Forest, Oregon

Earl's Sauna

He never talked about wanting anything.
He talked about his garden, his bees.
But if you sat in his sauna
on a wintery afternoon,
a whole world would open up,
and you would see his words
spin into desire as snow fell
past the window. You'd learn
to say the fire's name was yours; learn
to take the heat into your lungs
past words, and dream
trees rooting down, bending above.
You'd learn to open your mouth wide
as a baby bird crying its first song;
you'd take that song and live
a long time. It would open your life
the way fire opens the tongue inside a log.
Listen, and you hear it still, the breathing
and all that hunger going up with it.

Sagle, Idaho

At Twenty

they began to dream beyond
the rushing home each day
to hurry off to bed and sleep
only to rise at dawn and again
begin the monotonous labor
of pouring concrete, or dragging
heavy boards from off the beds
of semi-tractor trailer trucks – plywood,
six-foot sheets, hoisted
and carried fifty yards
to footings poured
the day before – foundations
for second homes in Idaho.
                So, one evening after work
they drove their company trucks
into the Payette Forest
to walk a while
amid the sound of wind
and falling leaves –
to walk along a ledge
and find a path to carry them
into the sulfur springs
        the Nez Perce had used
to rejuvenate themselves
and turn their lives outward
into the opening of dreams.

        Here, without hesitation
or need to talk, the laborers
unbuttoned their shirts

and blouses; they unzipped
their concrete-splattered jeans
and slipped into the steaming pools.

    *

And when they returned
to work the following day,
it was as some had feared –
a fellow employee,
having seen them
the night before
pulling off the road
away into the mountains,
forced them now to admit
their wayward indiscretions. *Yes
they had broken rules –
had used the trucks
for impermissible purposes –*
and now would walk home
bereft of jobs –
                but O
the gladness in their legs
to remember their bodies
unburdened
and dripping with light –

to see again the steam
unfurl around them
as they stood from the water
and began to gather their clothing –

shirts and blouses grown
into Trumpet lilies
spilling from their arms
as they planted their feet
         and tramped away
into a night of stars,
completely drenched.

Talking to Water

for MW

You show up laughing –
a plant in the mind's wind,
gripping tight to the ground –
a profusion of color,
a wheat field in summer,
fields around a house.

You want my eyes to stay on the canvas
while you disappear
through the smouldering clouds
leaves make burning under
the jack-o-lantern sun.

*

I'm talking to water.
I'm expecting you to appear
as you once did on stage: a swan dying –
you'd practiced and practiced
until it was perfect – and
the audience hushed into sorrow,
forgot all else breathing
around them.

But I am not hushed, nor forgetful.
I take your eyes into the light
at the tip of my brush.
I paint the heat I remember
flaring out around the outermost
edge of wing. I paint waves

curling beneath, ready to leap
to the fury your disturbance creates
in the ebullient waters of the mind.
This I stroke with love, a leave-
taking of symphonic proportions.

Go, mad and gentle love
and never look back,
unless it is to visit like this. Then come
as flight, pass through dreams and shred
illusion, show me the shimmering
I long to see your beauty beyond.

Shi Shi Beach, Olympic National Park, WA.

Dream Song

for Nelson Bentley, in memory

Do you think the fire will catch?
He wanted to know
and asked the student again
until the student gave
undivided attention
to the smoldering coals.

The student wanted to answer
the question that had become
a lifted wing inside of him
and yet before he could do this,
the man was crowding in,
encouraging the coals again, reaching
over to lift a twig
from off the forest floor
and using it
to conduct the coals
away from silence
into a hymn
      because he felt
the embers capable
of lifting into song – *Voice
over the coals of voice*, he sang

until the student rose
up through the melody
into the morning – awake
to the singe and taste
of words
his teacher long ago sang.

Watching the Dancers Carrying Their Shoes Home

They waded into the bending grass –
feet heavy, heads lowered.
They moved way from a man
shouting from a doorway
threats against their failing to learn
music into their bodies.

But they were done listening
the wind said when it lifted their hair,
for there they were with nothing
but the sudden surprise that had them
shrieking into the afternoon – cries

like water off a high ledge – cascading
into a free-fall and splashing
into the calmest of pools, pools
that spread into the luxuriant

glory of waters, gathering
every shade of leaf and tree
into themselves, and when a bird flies over,
that too, of course, must find its way
into the patterning that is constantly
remaking itself upon the waters
into a picture of fluidity and motion.

And that is how it is when I hear them
breaking out into their laughter, the six dancers,
laughing in a way that brings the park alive into all
that sparked it – this goofy, loud, gut-busting,
laughter, the dancers can't keep

from sharing with us now as we turn
away from conversations and sandwiches
to stare at them and wonder – smile even –
as they drop to their knees and disappear
into the grass, still laughing, as they search
for shoes they dispatched so irresponsibly.

In Reply to the English Professor Who Warned His Teaching Assistants Never to Date a Student, Ever, and Quoted Benjamin Franklin: 'The Most Important Thing is Being Virtuous, the Second Most Important Thing is Giving the Appearance of Being Virtuous.'

I'm going out to the movies with this woman
who is really so beautiful you must forgive me
if I have a fiancée, for she
lives far away, and I will not
see her yet for some time.
You must forgive me if you are a student
and realize this woman was once my student.
It's no use my saying it's not the way
it appears, appearance here is true and more
beautiful for that alone than anything
I might say defending myself.
No, stand warned, we are stepping out
and if this very night you see us
so happy and charged to be together, sparking,
say we are beautiful and virtuous
so far as we are able and courageous enough
to face a world that would have us otherwise.

Small Beer

for Tod Marshall

I can't believe in art with all my life.
What, to be a Michelangelo?
Who at the end of his life saw it all
differently – art as vain pursuit,
keeping him away
from hearing what he wanted to hear
most deeply in his hands, the shaping
force of his God's presence.

No, there are more important things
though it's hard for us to see that always.
We're jazzed with the hype of commitment,
belief, and dedication. Sure a vocation,
a calling, and we want to respond with our lives,
but art should be exactly beyond
designs we would force it to take.
Give me the wild horse there,
galloping through the desert
and let no rope ever so much as graze
the sleek perfection of her neck.
Let the pounding of hoofs be
the echo we train our ears to.
Let the clouds of dust popping
into extinction teach us
how to honor our late master
and learn what he was saying all along.

Vocation

for Cid Corman, in memory

The dark is test to see
which way you'll jump
or if you'll jump at all
away from heart.
The dawn will come
but what dawn upon?
Will it find you holding fast,
or losing grip? *This*
could be a distraction, or *that* –
something giving you cause
to look away from truest life. Temptations
carry us around the block
before we notice
we've left home. Listen,
I'll give you a clue –
stay with the desire opening
your heart each day. Look
for patterns in the weather
and make yourself familiar
with local geography –
become the salmon
that knows the river
by smell alone
and then one day
all I'm telling you shall fall
to history –
the disbelieving side
responsible for sending you out
on one empty errand after another
in search of every other green pasture

will be in front of you –
no pasture at all – but forest
burning and collapsing
into a showering
of spark and ash
that leaves the path ahead,
and you alone upon it,
illuminated
in the confident belief
of your own task.

Leaving a Forest

Those are my parents
walking through the forest
ahead of me and down
along the river, the forest
they taught me to enjoy
and find my way through.
I know that if I stop,
they'll continue on
until they reach the artist,
who paints light so perfectly
into the water
they almost feel they know
how deep the water is.
I know if I stop,
beneath the leaning oak
the yellow leaves falling
through the light
will be canvases
for shadow and time to paint
their finishing touches upon.
I know if I stop,
I'll see my parents stepping
over a tired footbridge
to reach the other side
and enter evening
beyond the blurring line
of cedar trees – a shroud
gathering into its hush
their quieting voices
until they become the forest –
all of it – this forest
they are leaving me.

II

in the water
is the image
is the traveler

    – Santōka

Ikebana

A fistful of lotus buds
soaking in a vase – ready
to open any moment now.

Omi-Ai

This woman has bad dreams
that keep her awake nights.
Sometimes she falls into a pit
of snakes she can't escape from.
Bad people, snakes in the grass, I'm telling her.
Maybe you're afraid of people, bad people – fears –
Maybe they are suitors?
And yes, she admits, maybe they are.

In another dream, she runs out of gas
and the car won't start.
She doesn't say any more than that.
She shuts up, afraid
she's already said too much, as if her words
might actually give body
to what she sees in dream.
She says she has other dreams
when her car won't stop,
no brakes at all, and goes
plunging down the hill over the edge
of a cliff she can't even see the bottom of
until her face is pressed right up against the glass,
and then there is nothing but impact.

I tell her I have dreams same too –
suppose everyone does –
we're fearful deep down,
and she thinks so too
and begins to cry
right there in the English lesson.

When I say maybe it means
she wants to be strong
and break away, at least
find a plausible way to defend herself
against her mother's insistence
she marry somebody, anybody,
soon as possible, she cries louder.

Along the Kamo

The old men play
shōgi and blow
petals off the board

In Praise of the Hot Japanese Summer

I love it when the women take off their clothes
in the hot, hot *mushi-atsui* heat of summer – shed them
and begin to show the more sumptuous
flesh the sun has gotten to early. Look
at her by the elevator there
wearing a cotton dress
and *zōri* with yellow flowers.
The dress's thin straps drip
so tantalizingly loosely
all your eyes can do is go on
to that darker skin around her shoulders,
and then plunge
to the perfectly pedicured feet,
the sizzling shock of red
toenail polish gleaming
into the subway's hazy light.

She's ready for something, Lord knows,
and when she catches your eye
this is the thought that registers:
among all the throngs of grey-suited businessmen
hurrying to work, you are the one
most taken by her, most
appreciative, most ready
to go to your knees and count your blessings
right there on the pavement,
at the altar her feet present.

To be so graced with the sight of her
in the early a.m. rush of traffic. O
let this be portent of things to come:

the Japanese summer unfolding
into one of those holy fans
designed to bring bountiful blessings,
good crops, and a healthy head of desire.

Though luck indeed you'll need today
for anything more to happen.
She's on her way, eyes darting,
this way and that, as she steps
onto the train and there
behind the window
looks to you
and then to the tissue
she dabs the glistening
beads of sweat away with
to send you on your way,
that, and her smile – enough
heat in these alone
to fire the cockles of any ageing man's heart,
say nothing of the city outside already ablaze.

No Hands

They pedal over a pathway
the farmers use for going out
to measure their barley, a pathway
used for generations
and worn into a sheet
of polished clay, so smooth
it reflects the sun
and becomes a mirrored stillness
the children glide over
without the least concern
for bumps along the way, traveling
into evening out there
where barley dips
and lifts into an ocean
of reddish gold, carrying
the laughter of children with it
until the pathway is only
a narrowing invitation
for eyes to tarry
and see the light go
flickering down
into the furrow of night
and growing quietness.

Girl on Fence

She wears an autumn uniform
and doesn't care a jot
about the teacher walking near
or the farmer racing towards her.
She's in some other world –
nine-feet tall and eating
the ready-for-the-market fruit.
She reaches up and snaps
the fruit from off the branch.
And when the farmer gets to her
to whack the fence
and scream her down,
she's already leaping away
and running farther
into the orchard, leaving him
beside the teacher
to count the wreckage strewn
upon the ground – the softening
cores of persimmons,
densely packed with seed
and listing towards the earth
where the teacher paces
and begins to pay attention
to what he feels
going on inside his legs
as he watches her run – a wound
of instruction, a song
that sends him into seeing
himself out there becoming
a little more audacious
and beautiful, as she is now

in running out the clock of day
and disappearing into it,
between the setting sun
and the opening stars.

Kusatsu, Shiga Prefecture, Japan

Learning Better

I

Beneath the blossoming plum trees
we wait once more for doors to open
so we may go inside and grade
another year of school exams –
who is   and who is not   to pass
through the hallowed gates in early Spring.

Was it Walter Payton last night
explaining his illness on television,
the several weeks he had to live?
Or was it video from Kosovo,
the discovery of so many
bodies in their shallow graves –

the boys and men of Srebrenica
unearthed along a mountain road –
        snow begining to fall
and women lining the road,
waiting in the cold and wind
to place their flowers close.

II

Last year between the grading of exams
we stood before the same doors
and spoke of Zen and Thomas Merton –
how he thought of spiritual practice
as mostly learning better how to die.

A year is gone and we confess
we haven't learned better how to die.
If we were Walter Payton today,
or boys from Srebrenica then –
guns pressed against our chests –
we wouldn't know better how to die.

III

We follow words into trees.
We see the silence they leave –
our words and then the scattering petals.

We see the blossoming branches
lift and sway and lull us
into a quiet fragrance, a fragrance

we know we are for now
breathing into our lungs
and breathing out again, wanting

the February blossoms, already
on their way to plums,
to be for us also trusted

emissaries
from *the world of emptiness*, here
among the living and the dying,

to offer softest word
touching
on continuance and becoming.

Ritsumeikan University, Kyoto

Hanami

Out for a day's viewing
and stopped by neighbor ladies –
far into their eighties –
who stand beneath the flowing
cherry blossoms to call,
'Come have a look!' – branches
they hold for us to see.

Kyoto

Visiting

Tonight the topic is 'dying,'
or more specifically,
what will become of their bodies?
Their faith is in the resurrection
but *the idea of being placed inside a casket…?*

The wake bothers my mother,
the idea of everyone staring at her
when she looks like *that!*
And my father?
He argues against the cemetery –
would rather be cremated –
doesn't understand the fuss
over a dead body, the expense of it.

My mother finishes her tea
and lifts her eyes
away from television –
she's off to bed.

And in the way she says *goodnight*,
in the way she bends to kiss our heads,
I know I'll need to fill her in tomorrow
when she leans over the coffee pot
and gives me that wide-open stare…

But father isn't talking.
He's easing into his *La-Z-boy*
and raising the remote
in search of something more interesting
than evening news
and record breaking snow, the snow

I watch outside the window
lifting into drifts
until a parachutist arrives,
struggling to stand
and bundle his gear,
the sheer and silken mass of chute,
into a small bag, a man
who stands as figment
inside the mind,
and yet a figment
helping me
to hear the other man
sitting in his *La-Z Boy*, calling out
to his wife – *Good night, love!* –
helping me to hear
how those words fall
into the familiar
order of their lives
as quietly as snow
falls through the night
and fills the surrounding mountains
with the approaching
white water rivers of spring.

Frosted pickle barrels
where you no longer live
stacked and empty

Treasure

for the children of Patayas

The mountain slides beneath her feet
as she climbs
higher
and starts to rummage
through cans and bottles
until she lifts a wooden hanger. Now

the camera angle changes
to focus on reporters
huddled along the mountain slope
to talk of plywood shanties
buried beneath the avalanche they saw
rushing down the mountain yesterday.

The reporters speak of missing children
and then they speak of numbers dead.
They speak until the child arrives
to stand with them, breathless
and drenching wet
but ready to answer questions.

The child speaks of family
and then she turns to what she's found –
        the *treasure* it is for her
and for her family too, as she lifts it
for all to see
how *beautifully it's painted gold.*

She wipes her face –
palms against cheeks –
both sides – and smiles
as beads of rain begin to run
and shimmer
along the river of her hair.

And when the camera pulls away
and she begins to grow
small and then smaller
beneath the growing mound of trash,
the last we see of her
is just her smile
              and waving hand –
the last we see
in turning television off
and getting set for bed,
      opening closet doors
and handing each other hangers
to put our clothes away upon

with greater care tonight perhaps
as we undress before mirrors,
and see again her smile
appearing out before us
in lights that flash across
our shadowed mirror, some
confusion in the harbor, a boat
we turn to see patrolling
the waters with sirens

turned low
and lights flooding out – touching
the small hands of lifting waves.

New World Manila Hotel

Hirosato

Haneda Airport, Tokyo, March 15, 2011

Eight years old –
name tag pinned
to his chest ヒロサト.
His look of being
a little scared
as jet engines whine
their way up.

One empty seat
between us –
he's never been this close
to a *gaijin* before
but leans over – asks,
in 日本語,
Where's the bathroom?

He is heading south
away from the zone –
escaping
like children years ago
sent out of Tokyo
when fire bombs rained
terror down.

He settles in –
adjusts his seat –
'Ready or not,' I say,
and he smiles
        past my English
he doesn't understand,
into the better language
we are finding between us.

Elegy for Autumn Gordon, 14 Years

Smoke above the chimney
curling in the wind
and the falling snow

III

walking on through
Hagi yes
Susuki yes

– Santōka

'*Hagi* is the common wild bushclover (*lespidezza*) found in earliest Japanese poetry and famously also in Bashō – *susuki* the far-flung pampas grass of Japan.' (Cid Corman's note from *Walking into the Wind, A Sweep of Poems by Santōka, Versions by Cid Corman,* Cadmus Editions, 1990.)

Throwing My Life Away

We who have found / love will also find / words for each other
— Cid Corman

He put his hands on my shoulders
and looked me in the eyes.
He said, *I don't know how to put it to you*
gently, so here goes,
to marry and go to Japan, man,
you're throwing your life away.

But life is meant – isn't it –
to be thrown away, finally
with both hands for love?

But I listened to him, I did.
I listened 'til I stood above the world,
nothing below but cool shifting shadows
I couldn't see through,
like sitting in a pine forest at dusk,
trying to distinguish deer
from the smoke of a neighbor's fire.

But now, I prefer to remember purple coneflowers
that burst the Illinois summer into bloom,
my father carrying me into the pasture,
guiding my hand towards things I could trust
with my own eyes – how to bear the meaning up
out of flowers into the light waiting
at the thin edge of a petal's history,
giving us chance to see
our cocooned world shattered
into what lies beyond our own reckoning.

What is Great

in loving you
is your willingness to let me come
close enough to be entirely
trusted by you as if
I were none other
than who I am, thus strangely
I become the man
I want to be with you.

Kae's Vision

I'm tired of trying to control everything
I want to happen in my life.
I want the baby to change that –
take what I am now and force it
into new possibilities.

I could have been more careful
but what is *careful* sometimes
but dis-ease distracting us
away from our longed-for hope
of living here and now.

When they wheel me through the delivery room doors,
I want to see light breaking
into our house, a thief
stealing the life we charted without a child
and lasering it a zillion pieces to Sunday,
no room untouched. I'll see stars
mixing with the gold glittering dust of illusion.

When they wheel me through the beautiful doors
I already see closing down
the what-might-have-been, don't laugh,
you'll be in the yard digging through debris,
searching for a clue you can't even imagine now
important: clear mirror
you'll hold and see our faces in
for the first time different,
whole, and new.

Walking Home

> *for my father, Jeremiah A. Dunne* (1927-2009)

Susuki grass so tall it conceals
the huge harvest moon.

What I see is the fluffy heads of seed
blowing into the cool pool of night air.

How splendid to see the stems sway
and feel the breeze move
down around the mountains, soft
as my daughter's breath stirring
loose from dreams.

This is not a road I ever imagined
I'd walk, road behind my house,
road through mountains in Japan
strung with paper lanterns.

Years slip through holes
we wear in our pockets,
falling like coins & jangling
their passing preciousness.

There are stars on the other side
where I've come
to see the moon hold sway
and my questions fall
into an ocean of grass
the fireflies burn and fade over.

Ten years in Japan;
I hear my parents singing
my name through the pine trees
and I'm lost in a forest,
looking for the source.

Japan has risen over my life like a moon.
Home can never be one place.
But these stars too,
these mountains,
these children whose eyes
are full of Japan, my children,
who reach through night and day
to hold me in the soft
enclosure of their illuminating love.

The Dance

for my son, one year old

Jyōji throws hands high,
yells, squats and turns
round and round, falls
with eyes smiling
everywhere at once –
shine, shine, shine.

Finders Keepers

I picked him off the floor where he lay crying
wrapped around your ankles at the sink
and kept on with the arguing –
his head resting on my shoulder
growing heavier as the words came
to me with ever increasing speed,
violence tipped with anger
at you for defying me – and on
we went, tearing the house down
as the weight grew heavier
in my arms, until it was too much,
screamed out, near hoarse,
I had to go to the couch
and lay our sleeping boy down
in a room grown suddenly small
enough for us to begin searching together
for the one blanket he wanted us to find.

Like a Poem

because 'Emi'
means three different things at once…
because the first syllable (恵) means blessing…
and the second syllable (美) means beautiful…
because a further reading in Japanese offers
niko-niko: 'smile,' which is to say,
the onomatopoetic evocation of the act,
the inner expression of
the sparkle of teeth, the feeling of delight…

because she's turning four years old today
and wears a summer dress
with a giant strawberry
floating in a bowl of cream
right there on her chest…

because she hears the hungry fish
all the way under
the shadows of the pond
and kneels to coax them up –
   the orange and red *koi* (鯉) –
to rise and feed
   a pinch of food for every gaping mouth…

because she bows
when all the food is gone…
because she turns
upon the grass
to do what fishes do
as they circle away and fade…

because she grows silent
and puts her hand in mine
to signal *time to go…*
because she believes
our shadows will stay
upon the waters
and float *this way forever…*

because she helps me feel
the fragrance of the afternoon
   slipping into evening
on leaves of bamboo,
   already wet with rain
as we turn
    'round and 'round to begin
            the shortest walk ever home.

Points of Departure

for David Jenkins, in memory

I

Taking Emi to school and glad –
The *privilege* you said it would be,
You who cherished walking
Mary to school each day.
Easy to remember the two of you
Walking past the house –
Mornings you splashed through puddles
And spoke the words
She loved to say,
Galoshes or *pinhead* or *nincompoop*.

You were forty-seven
When fatherhood arrived –
*The best thing
In all the world to happen.*
I was thirty-seven
Scared and far from sure
When you talked with me
Late into an evening
In April – helped me
See the event
As life opening beyond
Expectations
Into joyful
Uncharted worlds
Of *first experiences
With many more firsts to come.*

II

Mary didn't look at us.
She stood during the memorial
And left the café – left
As soon as she noticed
We planned to play
A recording of you
Reading your translations.

She slipped away
In school uniform
With a book of *manga*
Pressed to her chest –
She went outside and sat
On a broken stool and rested
Her head against the glass.

You would have enjoyed
Seeing the way the book
Brought her a smile –
The way her breath
Fogged the glass
into the shape of a dancer.

You would have loved
The blossoms falling
Through the darkness – lamplight
Catching every tilt of leaf.

But mostly, my friend,
You would have loved to see
Your daughter finding her place
To be with you – out there
On her own terms –
Not needing a recording
To be with you there
In the quiet companionship

of her book and the falling blossoms.

Skylight

Because she prays one way
and her husband prays a different way,
a different faith, *it follows,*
the doctor on CNN is telling the world,
their children will be confused.
When I turn the television off,
it's early morning in Japan.
I'm walking through the dark bumping
first into the table and then the chair
before reaching the door and sliding it open
to find my family on the floor
asleep beneath futons
that lift around their breathing
and stretch away under the moon like waves.
We are of different faiths and races,
our nationalities are different too, and yes,
I could remain awake for hours
to toss and turn around the news
of what awaits our children
but thankfully I have these stars
and children sleeping soundly
their faces turned toward the light
that travels through the universe
to be with us so perfectly confused.

Drifting

> *for John Keeble*

To wake with a kind of grace
and not feel harried – how easy
to be swept off into the current
of life's demands…
I'd rather be more able
to drift into seasons,
to attend projects and chores
with eyes ready for the least
disturbance any blade of grass
turning in the wind can make –
to be a hunter who realizes
the fullness an instant offers – to accept
here and now the unexpected
gift of learning how it is
to let disturbance enter you
and turn you out towards its life –
then I might be more able
to be the man I want to be –
the father lifting his children free
from fear of disturbing his day
or breaking his holy train
of concentration. Here, I am.
I'm pounding down the stairs.
I'm running through the kitchen
to see what's happening *this time*.
and there they are – the children,
too scared to say a word

of how the vase was broken –
    only their tears
and open arms
to guide me past the shattering
into the station of this attentiveness.

Home Test

for Airi

The world looks different
when you come home from work
and your wife meets you at the door
with one of those sticks she holds in the air
as if she were a diviner out looking for water,
or maybe someone testing to see
which way the wind is blowing. Today
it's gale-force catches our sails – that stick
reading she's positive for pregnancy again –
Home Test, and now showing me the line
running down the center, luminous and alive
with a future we are tending towards. Her eyes,
large with alarm or playful disbelief, show me
the hope and expectation below,
and how she loves the moment
she breaks the news and watches me spin
into my worries of *Whoaaa –*
How are we going to manage THREE? And yet
before I spin so far as that, I'm with her
on the floor of our living room braced
for all we feel sweeping through us – this clearing
instant of change that leaves us marooned
upon the shores of our being here
with each other in the quiet surprise
that hits like a wave and leaves us
stretched out into it – this new world
we feel for the first time we are meeting.

First Day

Bigger than most, she's sitting pretty
looking alert – her hair done up
in a pony tail. She's wearing her uniform
and stretching the skirt beneath herself
the way a lady would. Younger kids,
two and three years-old, march
past outside the window. Now,
from out behind her calm countenance
come the welling tears she quickly
brushes aside with her fingers.
I want to go to her but know
I must stand away. All I can do
is smile from the back of the room, this room
I am beginning to take the measurement of –
call it *fatherhood* from here on out. But already
I have her tears in my eyes, too,
it works like that and she sees this and chokes
into a sobbing that seems to rush between us
like a river we can neither get across
nor meet in the middle of – at least not until
she turns to face the teacher, and I,
on my side, turn to face this dearest song
I think I've ever heard, lifting into my heart
light and airy as the blossoms streaming
from the trees in the yard and pouring
into the afternoon heat their small sweetness.

Yokkaichi, Japan

Notes

NOTES

FERRIS WHEEL is for Belinda Mata.

AT TWENTY is for Lisa Lombardi and David Peckham.

OMI-AI refers to the practice of arranged marriage in Japan.

ALONG THE KAMO: The Kamo river in Kyoto; 鴨川 (*kamo-gawa*) translates as 'duck river'. *Shōgi*, a Japanese form of chess.

IN PRAISE OF THE HOT JAPANESE SUMMER: *mushi-atsui* translates as 'steamy hot'; *zōri* are flat, thonged Japanese sandals made of rice-straw or other materials.

SMALL BEER: The poem takes its title from a remark by W. H. Auden: 'In the end, art is small beer. The really serious things in life are earning one's living so as not to be a parasite and loving one's neighbor. My vocation is to write poetry, but one mustn't overestimate its importance.' This poem is dedicated to the poet Tod Marshall, who studied alongside of me in a semester-long graduate course in Michelangelo's art.

LEARNING BETTER is for for the dead of Srebrenica (1995) and for Walter 'Sweetness' Payton, (1954-1999). 'Sweetness' Payton was a Hall of Fame American football running back who played for the Chicago Bears; he was given his nickname because of his kind and gentle nature. The phrase 'emissaries from the world of emptiness' makes use of an idea from a lecture on 'emptiness' by the Zen Buddhist teacher Shunryu Suzuki (1904–1971), as recounted in *Not Always So*, edited by Edward Brown, Harper-Collins, 2013. In his lecture Suzuki Roshi explains emptiness in the following way:

'We have a term, *shōsoku*, which is about the feeling you have when you receive a letter from home. Even without an actual picture, you know something about your home, what people are doing there, or which flowers are blooming. That is *shōsoku*. Although we have no actual written communications from the world of emptiness, we have some hints or suggestions about what is going on in that world – and that is, you might say, enlightenment. When you see a plum blossom, or hear the sound of a small stone hitting bamboo, that s a letter from the world of emptiness.'

TREASURE: On July 11, 2000, a landslide on a garbage dump in Patayas, Manila, killed 218 people, including children, who were living on the dumpsite. Witnesses, however, claim that the number of deaths is almost certainly much closer to 1,000.

HIROSATO: On March 11, 2011, The Great Fukushima Earthquake struck Japan. Dangerous levels of radiation leaked from the nuclear reactors at Fukushima causing the Japanese government to declare affected regions 'evacuation zones.' Many children were evacuated at this time and flown to safer regions of the country.

ELEGY FOR AUTUMN GORDON, 14 YEARS is for Autumn Gordon who loved blueberry pancakes and reading in bed on Sunday mornings with Philip, her father, and with her brother and sister. She was killed when a drunk driver drove head-on into the car she was coming home in from a swimming lesson.

LIKE A POEM: The poem refers to Hyakusaji Temple, Omihachiman, Shiga Prefecture, Japan. For Emi Kikuchi-Dunne and Robert Aiken. The definition of *niko-niko*, is taken from the late Robert Aiken's *A Zen Wave, Basho's Haiku and Zen* (Weatherhill, 1979).

POINTS OF DEPARTURE is for the late David Jenkins and his family: his wife Shinko and their daughter Mary Jenkins. David was a poet and a translator of Japanese classical literature. Along with Yasuhiko Moriguchi, his co-translator, he published the following books: *The Hojoki: Visions of a Torn World* (Stone Bridge Press, 1996); *The Dance of the Dust on the Rafters: Selections from the Ryojin-Hisho* (Broken Moon Press, 1989); *Simmering Away: Songs from the Kanginshu* (White Pine Press, 2006); *The Gates of Night* (Grey Spider Press, 1992).

§

COVER IMAGE: *The Red Line* by Sarah Brayer comes from her Red Thread Series of prints and is made from Tengujo washi, a thin mulberry paper that resembles silk. She notes, 'The red thread represents passion or energy moving through form. Zen master Ikkyu named a certain practice Red Thread Zen, in which passion could be a road to enlightenment.' (http://sarahbrayer.com/gallery/the-red-thread/).

§

Grateful thanks are due to the editors of the magazines where over the years many of these poems, or earlier versions of them, first appeared: Alan Botsford (*Poetry Kanto*), Thom Caraway (*Rock & Sling*), John Einarsen, Ken Rodgers and Robert Brady (*Kyoto Journal*), Richard Jones (*Poetry East*), Suzanne Kamata (*Yomimono*), Emily Rosko (*CrazyHorse*), James Shea and Kyoko Yoshida (guest editors of the Japan special issue of *Cha: An Asian Literary Journal*), and Phyllis Walsh (*Hummingbird*).

www.ingramcontent.com/pod-product-compliance
Lightning Source LLC
Chambersburg PA
CBHW031211090426
42736CB00009B/868